A Note from the Author

This book is dedicated to all the passionate individuals who strive for excellence in software quality assurance.

To the tireless testers who meticulously uncover defects, ensuring that every software product meets the highest standards of functionality and reliability.

To the diligent quality assurance professionals who craft comprehensive test strategies and plans, ensuring that no stone is left unturned in the pursuit of quality.

To the dedicated analysts who diligently document use cases and test scenarios, ensuring that software systems are thoroughly tested from every angle.

To the skilled scripters who automate testing processes, enhancing efficiency and accuracy, and enabling rapid iterations.

To the meticulous data managers who curate and maintain the essential test data, enabling robust and realistic testing scenarios.

To the vigilant defect managers who track, prioritise, and resolve issues, ensuring that software systems are continuously improved.

To the insightful testers who analyse test evidence, providing valuable insights and recommendations for quality enhancement.

To the diligent authors of Test Closure Reports, who document the journey, lessons learned, and achievements, ensuring knowledge transfer and continuous improvement.

This book is a tribute to your unwavering dedication, attention to detail, and commitment to excellence. May your passion for software quality assurance continue to drive innovation and elevate the standards of the industry.

Introduction

In today's fast-paced and continuously evolving digital landscape, delivering high-quality software products and services is paramount for businesses to achieve success. To ensure the reliability, functionality, and user satisfaction of software systems, organisations rely on robust Quality Assurance (QA) practices. This book, "Mastering Software Quality Assurance: A Comprehensive Guide," serves as your ultimate companion in understanding and implementing effective QA methodologies.

We will explore the foundational principles of Quality Assurance. We will delve into the importance of QA in the software development lifecycle, its role in ensuring customer satisfaction, and the key components of a successful QA process. By grasping these fundamentals, you will gain a solid understanding of the significance of QA and its impact on software development projects.

Building upon the QA fundamentals, the book focuses on developing a robust Test Strategy and Test Plan. We will explore how to define testing goals, identify appropriate testing techniques, establish entry and exit criteria, and create a comprehensive test plan that aligns with the project objectives. You will learn how to effectively prioritise testing activities and allocate resources, ensuring maximum test coverage while optimising time and effort.

We will discuss the process of capturing and analysing use cases, as well as translating them into effective test scenarios. You will learn how to identify and prioritise test scenarios based on business needs, user interactions, and system dependencies, resulting in comprehensive and targeted testing.

We will explore techniques for designing clear, concise, and traceable test cases that cover all functional and non-functional requirements. Additionally, we will discuss best practices for developing efficient and reusable test scripts that automate repetitive testing tasks, increasing productivity and reducing the potential for human error.

The availability of reliable and representative test data is crucial for thorough testing. We will examine strategies for identifying, generating, and managing test data that adequately covers various scenarios. Furthermore, we will delve into the importance of maintaining comprehensive test evidence, ensuring traceability, and supporting effective defect management processes.

Defect management is an integral part of the QA process. We will explore methods for efficiently capturing, tracking, and prioritising defects, as well as establishing effective communication channels between stakeholders. Additionally, we will discuss the importance of a well-documented Test Closure Report, which summarises the testing activities, results, and lessons learned throughout the project lifecycle.

In conclusion, "Mastering Software Quality Assurance: A Comprehensive Guide" provides you with a holistic understanding of Quality Assurance and its various components. By following the principles, strategies, and best practices outlined in this book, you will be equipped to deliver high-quality software products, meet customer expectations, and drive organisational success.

The Author

Julian Cambridge was born in London, UK.

- M.Sc. Business Computing
- B.Sc. (Hons) Computing with Business

Julian founded Golden Agile Solutions to supply IT consultancy activities to clients.

- Accredited Kanban Trainer (AKT, KMP, TKP)
- Certified Scrum Professional (CSM, CSPO, A-CSM, A-CSPO, CSP-SM)
- ICAgile Authorized Instructor (Agile Fundamentals, Agile Product Ownership, Agile Testing, Business Agility)

Quality Assurance

Quality Assurance (QA) refers to the systematic processes, methods, and activities implemented to ensure the achievement of quality in software development. It involves the planned and systematic activities that are focused on preventing the occurrence of defects and ensuring that the software meets the specified requirements and standards.

The key objectives of QA are:

1. Establishing standards and processes: QA defines a set of standards and processes for software development and testing to ensure consistency and quality across projects. This includes defining coding standards, documentation guidelines, testing methodologies, and quality metrics.

2. Requirement analysis and validation: QA teams work closely with stakeholders to understand their requirements and expectations. They validate the requirements to ensure they are clear, complete, and feasible.

3. Test planning and strategy: QA involves creating a comprehensive test plan that outlines the testing scope, objectives, resources, and timelines. It also includes

defining the overall test strategy, including techniques, tools, and environments to be used.

4. Test case development: QA teams create test cases based on the defined requirements and test objectives. Test cases are designed to cover different scenarios and validate the software's functionality, performance, security, and usability.

5. Test execution and defect management: QA involves executing test cases to identify defects or issues in the software. Defects are logged, tracked, and managed throughout their lifecycle until they are resolved.

6. Continuous improvement: QA aims to continuously improve the software development and testing processes. This involves analysing test results and defect data to identify areas for improvement, implementing corrective actions, and preventing the recurrence of similar issues in the future.

7. Collaboration and communication: QA fosters collaboration and communication among all stakeholders involved in software development, including developers, testers, business analysts, and project managers. Regular meetings, reviews, and feedback sessions ensure that everyone is aligned towards achieving the desired levels of quality.

8. Risk management: QA identifies and manages risks associated with software development. This involves assessing risks, developing risk mitigation strategies, and taking proactive measures to prevent potential issues.

9. Compliance with standards and regulations: QA ensures that software development processes and products adhere to relevant industry standards, regulations, and best practices. This is particularly important for applications that involve sensitive data, such as healthcare or financial systems.

By implementing effective QA practices, organisations can reduce the number of defects, improve customer satisfaction, enhance the reliability and performance of software applications, and increase the overall efficiency of the development process. QA plays a crucial role in ensuring that a high-quality product is delivered to end-users.

Test Strategy

A test strategy is a high-level plan that outlines the approach and methodology for testing a software application or system. It provides guidance on how testing will be conducted, the types of tests that will be performed, the resources and tools required, and the timeline for testing activities.

Here are some key elements that should be included in a test strategy:

1. Objectives: Clearly define the goals and objectives of the testing effort, such as identifying defects, evaluating system performance, or ensuring compliance with requirements.

2. Test Levels: Specify the different levels of testing that will be performed, such as unit testing, integration testing, system testing, and acceptance testing. Define the scope and objectives for each level of testing.

3. Test Types: Identify the different types of tests that will be conducted, such as functional testing, performance testing, security testing, usability testing, or regression testing. Determine the priority and schedule for each type of test.

4. Test Environment: Define the test environment requirements, including hardware, software, and network configurations. Ensure that the test environment replicates the production environment as closely as possible.

5. Test Data: Determine the test data requirements, including the creation of realistic and representative test data sets. Consider the need for data privacy and security.

6. Testing Tools: Identify the tools that will be used to support testing activities, such as test management tools, test automation tools, load testing tools, or defect tracking tools.

7. Test Schedule: Create a timeline for the testing activities, including milestones, deliverables, and dependencies. Determine the duration and sequence of each testing phase.

8. Test Resources: Allocate the necessary resources for testing, including the testing team members, their roles and responsibilities, and the skills and expertise required. Consider the availability of subject matter experts or external consultants.

9. Test Risks: Identify the risks associated with testing, such as schedule delays, resource constraints, or

inadequate test coverage. Develop mitigation strategies and contingency plans to address these risks.

10. Exit Criteria: Define the criteria for test completion and test closure, such as the number of defects remaining, the test coverage achieved, or the stakeholders' approval. Establish the conditions under which testing can be considered successful.

It is important to note that the test strategy should be flexible and adaptable, allowing for adjustments based on the project's evolving needs and requirements.

Test Plan

A test plan is a comprehensive document that provides a detailed description of the approach, scope, objectives, and deliverables of the testing effort for a specific project or software release. It is derived from the test strategy and serves as a roadmap for the testing team to follow.

A typical test plan includes the following components:

12.   Introduction: Provide an overview of the project and the purpose of the test plan. Include information about the software under test, its features, and the intended audience.

2. Test Scope: Define the boundaries and limits of the testing effort. Specify what will be tested and what will not be tested, including the testing levels, types, and environments.

3. Test Objectives: Clearly state the goals and objectives of the testing effort. This could include finding defects, validating functional requirements, evaluating performance or usability, or ensuring compliance with regulatory standards.

4. Test Approach: Describe the overall strategy and methodology for testing. This should include details on test design techniques, test prioritisation, and defect management.

5. Test Schedule: Provide a timeline for the testing activities, including key milestones, deadlines, and dependencies. This helps to ensure that the testing is completed within the project timeline.

6. Test Deliverables: Specify the documents, reports, and artifacts that will be created during the testing process, such as test scripts, test data, test logs, test cases, or defect reports.

7. Test Environment: Detail the hardware, software, and network configurations required for testing. Ensure that the test environment is representative of the production environment to obtain accurate results.

8. Test Data: Define the test data required for testing various scenarios. Specify how the test data will be obtained, created, or modified, and consider the need to protect sensitive or personal data.

9. Test Resources: Identify the resources required for testing, including the roles and responsibilities of each team member, their skill sets, and any training needs they might have. Also, specify any external resources or tools needed.

10. Test Risks and Mitigation: Identify potential risks and issues that may affect the testing process, such as resource constraints, dependencies, or technical challenges. Provide contingency plans or mitigation strategies to address these risks.

11. Exit Criteria: Define the criteria for determining when testing is considered complete, such as the number of critical defects remaining, the test coverage achieved, or the stakeholders' approval.

12. Approval: Specify the process and criteria for obtaining approval for the test plan from relevant stakeholders.

It is important to review and update the test plan regularly as the project progresses to ensure that it remains relevant and aligned with the evolving needs and objectives of the testing effort.

Use Cases

Use cases are detailed descriptions of how users interact with a system or software application to achieve specific goals or complete specific tasks. They outline the various steps and interactions between the user and the system, from the user's perspective. Use cases help in understanding the functional requirements of the system and provide a clear understanding of the system's behaviour.

Use cases typically include the following components:

1. Use case ID: A unique identifier for each use case, which aids in tracking and referencing.

2. Use case name: A descriptive name that identifies the purpose or objective of the use case.

3. Actor: The role or persona interacting with the system to accomplish a specific task or goal. Actors can be users, external systems, or other entities.

4. Description: A brief overview of the use case and its objective or business goal.

5. Preconditions: Any initial conditions or prerequisites that must be satisfied before the use case can be initiated.

6. Main flow: The step-by-step sequence of interactions and actions that the user or actor takes to accomplish the task or goal. This typically includes user actions, system responses, and expected outcomes.

7. Alternate flows: Branching paths or alternative actions that may occur during the use case due to exceptional or alternate scenarios. These scenarios cover exceptional situations, error handling, or alternate user choices.

8. Postconditions: The state of the system or any specific actions or outcomes that should occur after the use case is successfully completed.

9. Extensions: Additional optional or alternative paths that can be taken during the use case, providing more flexibility or choices to the user.

Use cases help in capturing the functionality of a system in a clear and concise way. They serve as a foundation for defining system requirements, designing user interfaces, and developing test cases. Use cases are also valuable for communication and collaboration between stakeholders, developers, and testers, ensuring a common understanding of how the system should function from the user's perspective.

Test Scenario

A test scenario is a high-level description of a specific functionality or feature of a system that needs to be tested. It outlines the conditions under which the testing will be performed and the expected behaviour or outcomes.

Test scenarios are broader in scope compared to test cases, as they encompass multiple test cases that cover different aspects or variations of the functionality being tested. They act as a bridge between the user requirements or business processes and the test cases that validate those requirements.

Typically, a test scenario includes the following components:

1. Scenario ID: A unique identifier for each test scenario to facilitate tracking and reporting.

2. Scenario name: A descriptive name that identifies the functionality or feature being tested in the scenario.

3. Description: A brief description of the test scenario, outlining the specific functionality or feature being tested.

4. Preconditions: Any initial conditions or prerequisites required for the test scenario to be executed, such as specific data or system configurations.

5. Test data: The specific input values or data sets to be used during the execution of the test scenario.

6. Steps: The sequence of actions and interactions that need to be performed to execute the test scenario, along with specific expected behaviours or outcomes for each step.

7. Expected results: The expected behaviour or outcome after executing the test scenario.

8. Actual results: The actual behaviour or outcome observed during the execution of the test scenario.

9. Pass/Fail status: Indication whether the test scenario passed or failed based on the comparison of the actual results with the expected results.

10. Notes: Any additional information, observations, or notes related to the test scenario, including any known issues or workarounds.

Test scenarios help establish an overall testing approach and provide a high-level view of the testing scope. They help ensure that all the relevant functionalities are covered by test cases and provide a framework for organising and prioritising the testing effort. Test scenarios also serve as a communication tool between stakeholders, testers, and developers, ensuring a shared understanding of the test coverage and expected outcomes.

Test Cases

Test cases are specific scenarios or conditions that will be tested during the software testing process to verify its functionality, performance, or other desired characteristics. They are designed to ensure that the software meets the specified requirements and works as expected.

Test cases typically include the following components:

1. Test case ID: A unique identifier for each test case to facilitate tracking and reporting.

2. Test case name: A descriptive name that identifies the purpose or objective of the test case.

3. Test case description: A detailed description of the inputs, actions, and expected results for the specific test case.

4. Test case preconditions: Any specific conditions that must be met before executing the test case, such as the availability of certain data or the completion of a specific task.

5. Test case steps: Step-by-step instructions on how to execute the test case, including the specific actions to be taken and the data to be entered.

6. Expected result: The expected outcome or behaviour of the software after executing the test case.

7. Actual result: The actual outcome or behaviour observed during the test execution.

8. Pass/Fail status: Indication whether the test case passed or failed based on the comparison of the actual result with the expected result.

9. Test case priority: The relative importance or urgency of a test case, which helps in prioritising the testing effort.

10. Test case status: The current status of the test case, such as "Not Started," "In Progress," or "Completed."

11. Test case dependencies: Any dependencies or relationships between test cases, such as the need for specific test data or the successful execution of previous test cases.

12. Test case notes: Any additional information, observations, or notes related to the test case.

It is important to design test cases that cover a wide range of scenarios, including both positive and negative tests, boundary cases, and edge cases. Test cases should be clear, concise, and unambiguous to ensure repeatability and consistency during testing. They should also be designed to validate the software against the specified requirements and to uncover defects or issues.

Test Scripts

Test scripts are detailed instructions or sets of commands that guide testers on how to execute specific test cases. They provide a step-by-step procedural guide to ensure consistent and accurate execution of the tests.

Test scripts typically include the following components:

1. Test script ID: A unique identifier for each test script to facilitate tracking and reporting.

2. Test script name: A descriptive name that identifies the purpose or objective of the test script.

3. Test script description: A brief description of the test script and the specific test case(s) it covers.

4. Test script steps: Detailed instructions for executing the test case, including the specific actions to be taken, data to be entered, and expected outcomes.

5. Test data: The specific data or input values to be used during the execution of the test script.

6. Expected result: The expected outcome or behaviour after executing each step of the test script.

7. Actual result: The actual outcome or behaviour observed during the test execution.

8. Pass/Fail status: Indication whether each step of the test script passed or failed based on the comparison of the actual result with the expected result.

9. Test environment: Details about the specific test environment configuration or settings required for executing the test script.

10. Test script dependencies: Any dependencies or prerequisites required for the successful execution of the test script, such as the completion of certain preconditions or the availability of specific test data.

11. Test script notes: Any additional information, observations, or notes related to the test script, including any known issues or workarounds.

Test scripts are typically created based on the test cases defined in the test plan. They serve as a detailed guide for testers to follow during the execution of the tests. Well-designed test scripts help ensure consistency, accuracy, and repeatability in the testing process and facilitate efficient defect identification and reporting.

Use Case, Test Case, Test Script example

Use Case:

Title: Making a Purchase Online

Objective: To simulate the process of making a purchase on an e-commerce website.

Actors: Customer, Website

Preconditions: Customer has a registered account on the website and has added items to their cart.

Main Flow:
1. Customer logs in to the website using their credentials.
2. Customer navigates to their shopping cart.
3. Customer selects the items they want to purchase.
4. Customer clicks on the "Checkout" button.
5. Customer fills out the billing and shipping address details.
6. Customer selects a payment method (e.g., credit card, PayPal).
7. Customer enters payment details.
8. Customer clicks on the "Place Order" button.
9. The system processes the payment.

10. The system displays a confirmation message with the order details.
11. The customer receives an email confirmation.

Postconditions: The customer's order is successfully placed, and they receive a confirmation email.

Test Case:

Title: Making a Purchase with a Credit Card

Test ID: TC001

Preconditions: Customer has a registered account on the website, has items in their cart, and is on the checkout page.

Test Steps:
1. Enter valid credentials and log in to the website.
2. Navigate to the shopping cart.
3. Verify that the selected items are correct.
4. Click on the "Checkout" button.
5. Fill in the billing and shipping address details correctly.
6. Select the payment method as a credit card.
7. Enter valid credit card details (e.g., card number, expiration date, CVV).
8. Click on the "Place Order" button.
9. Wait for the system to process the payment.

10. Verify that a confirmation message is displayed, containing order details.
11. Check the customer's email for a confirmation email.

Expected Results:
- The customer should be able to log in successfully.
- The correct items should be displayed in the shopping cart.
- The billing and shipping address details should be correctly filled.
- The credit card should be accepted for payment.
- A confirmation message with the order details should be displayed.
- The customer should receive a confirmation email.

Test Script:

Test Case ID: TC001

Test Steps:
1. Go to the website's login page.
2. Enter valid username and password.
3. Click on the "Login" button.
4. Go to the shopping cart page.
5. Verify that the items in the cart match the expected items.
6. Click on the "Checkout" button.
7. Fill in the billing and shipping address fields with valid information.
8. Select the payment method as a credit card.

9. Enter valid credit card details.
10. Click on the "Place Order" button.
11. Wait for the system to process the payment.
12. Verify that a confirmation message with the correct order details is displayed.
13. Check the customer's email inbox for a confirmation email.

Expected Results:
1. The login page should load correctly.
2. The username and password should be entered without any errors.
3. The login should be successful, and the user should be redirected to the account page.
4. The shopping cart page should load without any errors.
5. The items displayed in the cart should match the expected items.
6. The "Checkout" button should navigate to the billing and shipping address page without any errors.
7. The billing and shipping address fields should accept valid information.
8. The credit card option should be selectable.
9. The credit card details entered should be without any errors.
10. The "Place Order" button should trigger the order placement process.
11. The system should process the payment without any errors.

12. The confirmation message should be displayed with the correct order details.
13. The customer should receive a confirmation email containing the order details.

Test Evidence

Test evidence refers to the documentation and artifacts that provide proof or verification of the testing activities and their results. It serves as a record of the tests conducted, the expected and actual outcomes, and any issues or defects found during the testing process. Test evidence is essential for traceability, compliance, and validation purposes.

Some examples of test evidence include:

1. Test cases: Test cases are specific instructions or steps that testers follow to validate the functionality of the software. They outline the inputs, expected outputs, and the steps to be executed. Test cases provide evidence of the tests performed and serve as a basis for reproducibility.

2. Test scripts: Test scripts refer to automated scripts that are used for executing automated tests. They contain instructions for the automated test tools to simulate user interactions, input test data, and verify the expected results. Test scripts can provide evidence of the automated tests executed and facilitate regression testing.

3. Test logs: Test logs capture the chronological record of the testing activities. They include details such as the

date and time of test execution, the test environment used, the test data employed, any actions performed, and the results obtained. Test logs provide evidence of the testing activities performed and can be useful in troubleshooting and root cause analysis.

4. Test reports: Test reports summarise the results of the testing activities. They include the test objectives, the test coverage, the test execution summary, and the identified defects or issues. Test reports provide evidence of the test results and serve as a communication tool with stakeholders.

5. Screenshots and videos: Screenshots or videos can be captured during the testing process to provide visual evidence of the tests executed and the observed behaviour or defects. They can be particularly useful in documenting visual issues or user interface problems.

6. Defect reports: Defect reports document the details of any issues or defects found during testing. They typically include information such as the defect description, steps to reproduce, severity, priority, and related artifacts. Defect reports provide evidence of the defects discovered and facilitate their resolution and tracking.

7. Traceability matrix: A traceability matrix is a document that maps the requirements or user stories to the corresponding test cases. It provides evidence of

how the testing is aligned with the requirements and ensures that all requirements are adequately tested.

8. Audit trails: Audit trails capture the history of changes made to the test artifacts, such as test cases, test scripts, or test data. They provide evidence of the changes made and enable traceability and accountability.

Test evidence is critical for ensuring transparency, accountability, and compliance in the testing process. It allows for effective reporting, tracking, and decision-making based on reliable and validated data.

Test Data

Test data refers to the set of specific inputs, conditions, and variables that are designed and used to execute test cases and verify the functionality, performance, and behaviour of a software or system under test. Test data is an essential component of the testing process and is used to simulate real-world scenarios, edge cases, and boundary conditions to ensure the thoroughness and accuracy of the testing activities.

Here are some key aspects related to test data:

1. Test data creation: Test data can be manually created or generated using automated tools. It should cover a wide range of scenarios, including positive and negative test cases, invalid inputs, boundary values, and concurrent or parallel operations. Test data may include different data types, sizes, formats, and combinations to ensure comprehensive test coverage.

2. Test data management: Test data should be organised, documented, and stored in a controlled and secure manner. It is important to manage and maintain the version control of test data to ensure consistency, traceability, and reproducibility of test results. Test data management tools and techniques can help in creating, tracking, and maintaining test data sets.

3. Test data independence: Test data should be independent of the production or live data to ensure the privacy and security of sensitive information. Test data should be carefully anonymised or encrypted to protect confidential data and comply with privacy regulations.

4. Test data validity: Test data should be valid and relevant to the testing objectives. It should accurately represent the expected data inputs and conditions that the software or system under test is likely to encounter in the real world. Invalid or incorrect test data can lead to inaccurate test results or false positives/negatives.

5. Test data variation: It is important to have sufficient variations in test data to cover different test scenarios and achieve proper test coverage. Variations can include different combinations of input values, boundary conditions, large data sets, and complex data structures. It helps in identifying potential defects and weaknesses in the system.

6. Test data traceability: Test data should be traceable to their source and associated requirements. This ensures that test cases are based on correct and up-to-date requirements, and any test outcomes or defects can be linked back to the specific test data used.

7. Test data maintenance: Test data needs to be updated and maintained throughout the testing

lifecycle. As the software or system under test evolves, test data may need to be revised, expanded, or modified to reflect changes in functionality, business rules, or data structures.

Effective test data management ensures that testing activities are conducted efficiently, accurately, and with a focus on critical scenarios. It helps in identifying defects, validating system behaviour, and ensuring the overall quality of the software or system under test.

Defect Management

Defect management, also known as bug tracking or issue tracking, is the process of identifying, documenting, tracking, and resolving defects or issues identified during software development and testing. It involves managing the entire lifecycle of defects, from their discovery to their resolution. Effective defect management is critical for ensuring the quality and reliability of a software application.

The key components of defect management include:

8. Defect identification: Defects can be identified through various sources such as testing, user feedback, or production environment monitoring. The defects are typically documented in a defect management tool or system.

2. Defect logging: When a defect is identified, it is logged into the defect management system. The defect should include sufficient information, such as description, steps to reproduce, severity, and priority, to enable developers or testers to understand and reproduce the issue.

3. Defect classification and prioritisation: Defects are typically classified based on their severity, impact, and

priority. Severity indicates the impact of the defect on the system or functionality, while priority determines the order in which defects should be fixed based on business or project needs.

4. Defect assignment and ownership: Once a defect is logged, it is assigned to the appropriate individual or team responsible for resolving it. A clear owner should be identified to ensure accountability and timely resolution.

5. Defect tracking and monitoring: Throughout the defect's lifecycle, its progress is tracked and monitored. This includes regularly updating the status, tracking the time taken for each stage (i.e., open, assigned, in progress, resolved, closed), and maintaining communication about any changes or updates related to the defect.

6. Defect resolution: When a defect is resolved, the fix is implemented by the development team. The resolution includes fixing the code, performing necessary testing, and verifying that the defect is resolved.

7. Defect verification and closure: Once a defect is resolved, it undergoes verification or retesting to ensure that the fix is successful and does not introduce new issues. When the defect passes verification, it is closed in the defect management system.

8. Defect analysis and reporting: Regular analysis of defects helps identify patterns, trends, and potential areas for process improvement. Defect reports are generated to provide insights into the overall defect status, progress, and effectiveness of defect management processes.

Effective defect management ensures that defects are addressed in a timely manner, minimising their impact on the end-users and the overall project. It helps in maintaining the stability and quality of the software application and provides valuable data for improving development processes in the future.

Test Closure Report

A test closure report is a document that summarises the testing activities and outcomes at the end of a testing cycle or project. It provides an overview of the testing process, the test results, and any lessons learned during the testing phase. The purpose of the test closure report is to formally close the testing phase and provide valuable information for future testing projects. Here are some key components typically included in a test closure report:

1. Introduction: This section provides an overview of the testing project, including the objectives, scope, and testing approach followed.

2. Test objectives: It outlines the specific objectives or goals of the testing phase, such as validating the software functionality, ensuring system performance, or verifying compliance with regulations.

3. Test coverage: This section describes the extent to which the software or system under test was tested. It includes information about the features, modules, or components covered by the test cases and any areas that were not tested.

4. Test results: The test closure report summarises the outcome of the executed test cases. It includes

information about the number of tests executed, passed, failed, or blocked. It may also provide details on any critical defects or issues identified during the testing phase.

5. Test deliverables: This section lists the various test artifacts and documents produced during the testing phase, such as test plans, test cases, test logs, and reports. It ensures that all necessary documentation is available for future reference.

6. Lessons learned: The test closure report includes a section on lessons learned during the testing phase. It outlines the challenges faced, best practices identified, and recommendations for improvement in future testing projects. These insights can help enhance the efficiency and effectiveness of future testing efforts.

7. Test closure criteria: Test closure criteria define the conditions that must be met to consider the testing phase complete. It may include aspects such as achieving a certain level of test coverage, resolving critical defects, or obtaining management approval.

8. Recommendations: The report may include recommendations for the project team or stakeholders based on the testing experience. These recommendations may suggest improvements for the software development process, testing methodologies, or tools used.

9. Sign-offs: The test closure report typically includes areas for stakeholders or project managers to indicate their approval or acceptance of the testing activities and outcomes. It ensures that all parties involved agree that the testing phase is complete.

The test closure report serves as a formal document to conclude the testing phase, communicate the results obtained, and provide insights for future testing projects. It acts as a reference for project documentation, decision-making, and auditing purposes.

Summary

Mastering Software Quality Assurance: A Comprehensive Guide" is a book that offers a comprehensive understanding and practical implementation of Quality Assurance (QA) methodologies in software development. The book covers various topics essential to QA, including Test Strategy, Test Plan, Use Cases, Test Scenarios, Test Cases, Test Scripts, Test Data, Test Evidence, Defect Management, and Test Closure Report.

The book begins by introducing the fundamental principles of QA and its significance in software development projects. It highlights the role of QA in ensuring customer satisfaction and outlines the key components of a successful QA process.

Subsequent chapters delve into specific areas of QA. The chapters on Test Strategy and Test Plan provides insights into defining testing goals, choosing appropriate techniques, prioritising testing activities, and optimising resource allocation. The chapters on Use Cases and Test Scenarios explores the process of capturing and analysing use cases, translating them into effective test scenarios, and prioritising them based on business needs.

The creation and execution of Test Cases and Test Scripts are covered in detail in a dedicated chapter. It discusses designing clear and traceable test cases and developing efficient and reusable test scripts for automation.

The importance of reliable test data and comprehensive test evidence is addressed in a separate chapter. It provides strategies for generating and managing test data and emphasises the significance of maintaining comprehensive test evidence for traceability and defect management.

Defect management, a crucial aspect of QA, is covered extensively in a dedicated chapter. It explains the process of capturing, tracking, and prioritising defects, as well as establishing effective communication channels between stakeholders. The chapter also highlights the importance of a well-documented Test Closure Report, summarising testing activities, results, and lessons learned.

In conclusion, "Mastering Software Quality Assurance: A Comprehensive Guide" equips readers with the knowledge and tools necessary to implement effective QA practices. By following the principles, strategies, and best practices outlined in the book, readers will be able to deliver high-quality software products, meet customer expectations, and drive organisational success.

Foundations of Scrum Agile

Education

£2.99

App Store

Google Play

Agile Development with DevOps

Agile Project Management: Navigating Pros and Cons of Scrum, Kanban and combining them

Communication Troubles of a Scrum Team

Disney's FastPass: A Queue Story

Introducing the Douglass Model for Agile Coaches

Kaizen: The Philosophy of Continuous Improvement for Business and Education

Mastering Software Quality Assurance: A Comprehensive Guide

Scrum: Unveiling the Agile Method

Testing SaaS: A Comprehensive Guide to Software Testing for Cloud-Based Applications

The Art of Lean: Production Systems and Marketing Strategies in the modern era

The Board: A day-to-day feel of life on a Kanban team

The Sprint: A day-to-day feel of life on a Scrum team

The Whole Game: Systems Thinking Approach to Invasion Sports